GOOD GRIEF, THE GROUND

WINNER, 21ST ANNUAL A. POULIN JR. POETRY PRIZE

SELECTED BY STEPHANIE BURT

GOOD GRIEF, THE GROUND

Margaret Ray

Foreword by Stephanie Burt

NEW POETS OF AMERICA SERIES NO. 49

BOA EDITIONS, LTD. ↳ **ROCHESTER, NY** ↳ **2023**

For information about permission to reuse any material from this book, please contact The Permissions Company at www.permissionscompany.com or e-mail permdude@gmail.com.

Publications by BOA Editions, Ltd.—a not-for-profit corporation under section 501 (c) (3) of the United States Internal Revenue Code—are made possible with funds from a variety of sources, including public funds from the Literature Program of the National Endowment for the Arts; the New York State Council on the Arts, a state agency; and the County of Monroe, NY. Private funding sources include the Max and Marian Farash Charitable Foundation; the Mary S. Mulligan Charitable Trust; the Rochester Area Community Foundation; the Ames-Amzalak Memorial Trust in memory of Henry Ames, Semon Amzalak, and Dan Amzalak; the LGBT Fund of Greater Rochester; and contributions from many individuals nationwide. See Colophon on page 112 for special individual acknowledgments.

Cover Design: Sandy Knight
Cover Art: Eleanor K. Ray
Interior Design and Composition: Isabella Madeira
BOA Logo: Mirko

BOA Editions books are available electronically through BookShare, an online distributor offering Large-Print, Braille, Multimedia Audio Book, and Dyslexic formats, as well as through e-readers that feature text to speech capabilities.

Cataloging-in-Publication Data is available from the Library of Congress.

NYSCA

BOA Editions, Ltd.
250 North Goodman Street, Suite 306
Rochester, NY 14607
www.boaeditions.org
A. Poulin, Jr., Founder (1938-1996)

For my family

We were sad on the ground.

—Jean Valentine

CONTENTS

ʀ

ʀ

FOREWORD

It's 2022. The world is ending, but how fast? and for whom? and what do we have to pay to keep it around for a little longer, just until we get that one last day with our kids, last hour of rolling around in bed (with or without someone else in the bed), last pancake, last walk, last book we love to read?

Good Grief, the Ground might be one of those last books: light enough to come back to us, and heavy enough to stay with it. It certainly feels "like the end of something" to Margaret Ray, who is—or writes as—a white, adult, American woman with Florida roots and a presence in New Jersey now, a teacher still close to the epoch of fortunate teens, for whom "no one/ is dead yet," teens full of hunger, "ready to go somewhere." What do we do with that hunger if we grow up, if we realize that some people are hungry for us, that some people are never full, that we too have needs we mistake for wants and vice versa, that two contradictory things can be true?

It's a book built for many of us to recognize ourselves, or else our cisgender sisters, our millennial cousins, our typical atypical co-workers' lives, whose "job is to be looked at." It's also a book by a poet who knows that she's white, and can write about it: a relief after how many generations of white writers who consider whiteness unmarked. It's a book about the real world, where words have meanings and references and some of the poems could almost be short stories, or slices from a memoir, except that they have the architecture and the engineering and the sharp edges and sparks-fly potential that inheres in true, real, memory-burrowing poems. Think Laura Kasischke, Lucia Perillo, the early Rita Dove, Wordsworth, George Crabbe. People are real and they rejoice and they hurt and they inhabit the lines and phrases that Margaret Ray assembles, "sitting in the bleachers for/ the JV boys' game before ours."

It's a world, the real one, where lots of other people—like the cheerleader for the Lady 'Canes—know something that the poet does not yet know, "and that was unforgivable." A world where (as in every world) "children are made of risk," and some of us try for them anyway, and many of us—not enough of us—want them to thrive. Against so many twentieth century hangovers who want poems that feel always and only "subversive" (or, worse yet, "revolutionary"), Margaret Ray sees injustice all around and understands how many of us want support, want somewhere to stand. We say to ourselves "you don't love me yet," and we wonder if we ever will.

Maybe Wanda will. She belongs among a generation of poets' alter egos, not the first (see the dramatis personae in Catie Rosemurgy, Caki Wilkinson, Maureen McLane, and more: yes, it's gendered: yes, everything's gendered), but among the strongest. She does science. She's an authority on something. She's self-possessed in a way that the chameleon poet in Ray herself can never be: that poet looks instead at the gory insides of bodies, the news from which we turn away, as from bad headlines or gored-open gators: "We gaze at their bodies and wander away/ to buy groceries, which is fine." "We leave a mess, don't we." Ray updates Frost's famous, or infamous, "'Out, Out—,'" itself a hot take on Wilfred Owen's "Disabled," and also Auden's most famous poem about a Brueghel in a museum.

What does Ray add to that trope in her dead-gator poem? Our American meme-based speech. The word "fine" (like the dog-in-a-dumpster-fire image that dominated our Trumpian years). The state of Florida. Most of all, "disorientation." It's not that (as in Frost, as in Auden, as in the men who knew their job descriptions for most of the previous century) we know how to turn away, but rather that we don't know, we're just flailing, there's blood on the road but we have to get home to put dinner on the stove.

Ray's line shape and line breaks reflect that disorientation: not order, not a chaos, but a way to keep the conversation going. Rime riche (repetition used as rhyme), the occasional full rhyme (the whole book ends on one!), list-making, long sentences punctuated by short ones. It's a book of recurring motifs, resuming lives, re-emergent things: look for the titular "ground." Look for the peaches. Above all, it's a book of speech sounds, not simply duplicated as in a transcript, but rendered: this is what it's like to try to talk about how it feels, what it's like to listen.

I could end there—that's enough, I think, to tell you why I want you to read this book, to buy a second copy for your best poetry-reading friend. I could but I won't, because "I am behind enemy lines and the line is adulthood." Me too, Margaret Ray, me too. Ray's work isn't just memorable: it's replicable, even memable. As with Frost, it makes you want to quote it, though (unlike Frost) Ray hasn't given up on us. "There were never any good exit strategies anyway." Rather than exit, exist. Get tethered together. Call peaches paradise. Don't wait for someone else's "analog relief." Pretend you're Wanda. Attend to the galaxy. Tend your garden. Listen to your younger self, your inner Artemis, as Ray does. Lie next to someone you like. See where it gets you. Stick around. Oh, and read on. You'll be glad you did.

—Stephanie Burt

The End of August

The beetles have gathered in pairs
at the tops of stalks of grass
to get in one last fuck before the fall,
and why not? This time of year I let the juice
run down my chin when I eat a peach, let it
merge with the river of sweat down
my chest, speak freely in the days before
I have to become, once more, at work,
Ms. Ray, who only rarely curses, covers
her shoulders, fine, keeps a part of me apart
while I play this role as if a roomful
of teenagers doesn't know the same thing I know,
which is that, despite the heat, the afternoon
shadows are longer than in June, and that
this feels like aging, like the end of something
every time it comes around. At home,
I move three-quarters of my mail directly
from the mailbox into the recycling bin. It's still
August, despite the creeping busyness; I'm still
forgiven for "not seeing" emails. It will be
a week before I sit down to read writing by
other people's children, to try to convince them
not to tell me what they think I want to hear,
as if they don't know they're made of
so many things besides words.
And now, over the drone of an administrator
at the end-of-summer faculty meeting,
a cicada, lazarus bug, must be perched
just on the windowsill, so loud it sings
outside this room, hissing its buzzing-
heat-made-into-sound call that means
here, here I am, come and love me, I die.

Haunt

It's after dark The girl and some others
are at the pool in one of the cinderblock
apartment complexes none of them live in
that caters mostly to university students
They have snuck in because this one
has a fence that's easy to climb and there's
a dark spot between streetlamps and it's
a small underused under-maintained pool
Oak leaves collecting in all the filters
They are seventeen It doesn't occur to them
they get away with this each time because
they are white There are five of them
held together by the loose ties of adolescence
and who has the keys to a beat-up car
They have done this before and they will
probably go on doing it but this is the last time
the girl is there with them not for any special reason
but because the summer is ending and they will
grow apart One of the boys is her sort-of
boyfriend The other two are his friends One
of their girlfriends is the other girl but the girls
are only aligned by this mutual association
with these boys who play a game called
There's gum on my fly but really it's some
of their sack they're pushing out through
a slit in the fabric to trick the girls into looking
at their balls The girls understand they are
supposed to let them do things like this
They are supposed to watch the boys jump
The girls swim a little in their underwear
but mostly they sit on the edge of the pool
dangling their feet It is sticky humid
late summer hurricane season in Florida
The girl's hair sticks to the back of her neck
and she laughs when it seems like she's supposed to

These boys are tiresome The other girl is bored
lighting a Swisher Sweet and touching base
with her own reflection in the dim water
They have driven across town for this These
are their waters and their watering place
They drink but what does it mean to be whole
They are confused confused They think the tricks
the boys do while diving into the pool are
for their benefit and not that one will die
in a drunk driving accident four years from now
which the girl will learn about on Facebook
Time spooling out from how little you know
when you're young When the others aren't looking
the girl scoops a frog out of the pool drain
The leaves are spinning in the eddy One boy
gashes his heel on the concrete executing a flip
Now there's commotion about blood in the water
Jokes about DNA evidence Time to clear out
He's really bleeding but he's laughing because
he wants to be a man and everyone's a little
tipsy The girl has frozen but the other girl
wraps her bandana around it and everything
is ok They're piling into the car and no one
is dead yet and the girl has that sensation
she keeps having of falling and falling and then
good grief, the ground, and it's made
of wet wind and something she won't be able
to name for years

Making Out at the Movies

After Frank O'Hara

There was always gum involved,
back row under the projector.

Sometimes I wanted to, sometimes
I didn't but let it happen anyway because

once you agreed, those were the rules.
Sometimes I "went to the bathroom"

and put a coin in the Pac Man machine
in the lobby instead, that dark,

confetti-print carpet smelling of stale butter,
the concession stand cashiers outside for a smoke

or leaning conspiratorially against
the counter, facing somewhere else,

I didn't care, away from me.
The boy had been brought up in church.

I hadn't, but that didn't save me
feeling shame all the time.

I was so absorbent. I remember
the smell of his saliva around my lips, scraps

of dialogue from whatever B-movie
we'd bought tickets to

because it would be mostly empty
and was playing at the right time.

God was everywhere but with me,
and I was superstitious.

Kids of America, let yourself go to *good* movies!
There are things you can absorb

without meaning to, like that you can tell sincerity
by its sound, or that protagonists

are mostly white, or that there are whole genres
where the woman evaporates

during the good parts, or that people usually know
what they want. After,

it was always a relief to emerge
from the over-airconditioned building

to thaw in the steamy Florida night, frogs
and insects setting up an electric throb

from the retention pond between the theater
and the strip mall. I could go home, then,

having played my part convincingly,
my face in the dark: screen, projector, dust.

Hail Mary

The gym at the rural high school
forty-five minutes outside of town,
no AC, just the giant fans set in the walls,
rotating lazily like B-52 propellers
warming up on the runway, slicing
up the sunlight as it hits the hardwood floor.
Smell of dust and resin
in the humid Florida afternoon.
In the locker room was where J told me
she was more than a week late and
worried she was pregnant.
Then she got eight rebounds
(though she was no taller than me and played wing)
and I thought about it every time I saw her
take an elbow in the gut.
I had always been the one who watched her
(not sure what it was I was looking for):
strong and fearless under the rim,
the way she'd throw her body to the floor
for a loose ball, and that day

she became, for me, a goddess
as she sat sweating on the locker room bench
at halftime, elbows on her knees,
a glow of danger and ferocity pulsing off her.
I don't think she'd told anyone else
but she wouldn't let me catch her eye
during the game, which we lost
when their point guard hit a buzzer-beater
from half-court, and on the bus back
she sat sleeping or pretending to sleep
under her hood, discman turned all the way up.
The way our lives could bend
around this thing—

that knowledge grew between us—a blade
we would have to carry later, mothering
ourselves, or anything that came along.

Expulsion Lessons but Replace the Garden with a Swamp

This is Florida, one of the places in America
onto which we like to map our fantasies:
garden-walled, movie-set-theme-parks in this
swampier, sadder sister of California.

I want to tell you about two events
that form the cusp of a childhood:
One thing happened to me (alone),
and one happened (on TV) to America
after it happened (in private) to a pair

of people I'll never meet. Maybe I
belong to a subset of my generation,
our sexual awakening timed to coincide,
in 1998, with the Clinton impeachment:

we learned what a blowjob was because it was what
the president did with someone named Monica Lewinsky
and everyone was talking about it on TV and off.
It wasn't until later that I understood the blue
dress, the stain, what they signified.

How you learn a language: immersion and time.
I'd wanted to understand,
so I held these words in my mouth.
Her mouth. His penis. Look how we change

when we can name things. Here's the second:
Two hours north of Disney World,
a middle-schooler nested in the couch
doing math homework, I felt
eyes on me through the window.

He was in the palmettos
right up against the house. Two
more years before I would be overcome
with shame, naming what he'd

been doing, looking at me, shame
for how I'd tried to describe it to my mother:
something pink, like an udder, like milking
a cow in fast-forward on the VHS.
Instinctively keeping it

from friends for years. Worrying
about windows. But this was Florida, land
of forgetting, and the windows are often
obscured with mildew or frogs or vines

or condensation. It was later, later,
once I took the memory off its shelf
and turned it over again, only
once I knew what he'd been doing
while he looked at me, that's

when I was no longer a child. I would know
and refuse to use the word *masturbate*
long before I had the colloquial *jerking off.*
But I had *peeping tom* before *voyeur.*

I had a middle-school-friend who is
one of the Ariels at Disney now, little
girl's dream. She sings in her bright red wig
six days a week, or sits on a float
in disguise, and her job is to be looked at.

One of those walled-in parks. I imagine
her swiping in, some back entrance,
a key card. I imagine she leaves her tail
in her locker, gets takeout

on the way home. Imagine
the mermaids walking among us. Think of all
the windows. Think of all you understand.
Are you hungry? Do you want some fruit?
Didn't you want to understand?
If you still want to, you can name all that.

Tourist

The great trouble in human life is that looking and eating are two differ-ent operations.
      - Simone Weil

She wants to eat god, so she goes
to the museum. She wants to gum
the wrist of the baby in the paintings,
especially when he is depicted as simply
a mini adult. She goes by the book,
the one in her backpack, and though she says
Greek to herself quietly, over and over,
Greek, Greek, here in this northern city
on a river nowhere near the Mediterranean,
she wants to sink her teeth into the folds
of white marble robe wrapped around
the headless female figure. She wants for
resistance, wants to stuff the hard consonants
of this foreign language into her mouth.
She goes to the cheese shop and looks,
goes to the butcher shop and looks at
the meats as they glisten and hang, wants
for transitive verb and object without
interposing preposition, so she goes
to the cathedral to eat the organ, goes
to the river to consume the architectural leftovers
of ancient commerce, wants to eat the word
architecture, she wants to taste the briny smell
of the hulls and the damp bodies of the people
in the bus wants to dry her tongue
on the felt of the seats wants to click her teeth
against the shiny red pole she hangs
on to, standing, while the bus jerks
all the bodies around corners. She
wants to bite down on the thick coins
in her pocket, carry them pinned

between molars, taste all the hands,
the hotel room key-card would fit
in her closed mouth, propping out her cheeks
like the x-ray bite-plate panel at the dentist.
When she meets her dark-haired host she
takes his hand, raises it to her lips.

A Collection of Dangerous Things Interspersed with Things Occasionally Fine or Good

It's not the way it hurts when the long-distance train rushes through the platforms that I miss but the feeling of being ready to go somewhere. So much learned shrinking. The gauntlets were never fewer, we just didn't have the internet. The dried or dying spots on my plants' leaves look like writing. I can sit still here and look like I'm trying. I can go wait on the platform, that's not a problem, it's any kind of arrival that's missing, sometimes buzzing. It's not the pile of unopened mail that makes me remember the way someone else used to take up all the space, but the way it feels to fling open the windows on the coldest day of the year. I've been shopping for ways to get out of here. There's always something that needs recycling. Tiny cuts all over my hands because it's winter and I've been breaking down boxes. It's winter and I've been breaking down. It's winter and I've been filling jars with vinegar and flies. I've been shopping for fruit, but online, where you can't touch anything before you bite.

Freezing the Meat

Chalk-white ice cube tray full
of something alarming-red and chunky.
This is what I pull out of M's freezer

on the first warm afternoon of April. She's slicing
a lime for our gin and tonics, I'm retrieving
the so-called ice, her four-week baby sleeps

in a basket on top of the nearby washing machine.
"Do you have any regular ice or should we
have raw steak-cubes in our drinks?"

Her threadbare, still twinkling laugh. A little
sheepish: read somewhere, also her doula mentioned,
supposed to prevent postpartum depression,

when she typed in *freezing the placenta*,
Google auto-suggested *for smoothies*, and here we are
in her kitchen: she's using the paring knife

to gesture while I stare down at this chopped
and portioned collection of her. Little violences
on ice. Before this visit, scavenging

my own freezer for an offering, I'd stared
at the nearly fleshless leftover chicken carcass,
thigh-bone the size of an infant's forearm.

Now I ask, "Where's your real ice?"
And M stabs the air at the freezer, meaning
back left. When I get home again later, I, too,

will Google *freezing the placenta for smoothies*,
find one woman's website with instructions plus pictures
(like a liver, if I knew what liver looked like. The heft

of an essential organ). A commenter
on the placenta-smoothie site worries
over a biblical prohibition against cannibalism.

Flicking through the images, I'll chew
the inside of my cheek just enough
to taste something coppery. In M's kitchen,

we clink glasses before, from the washer,
her little death machine begins to cry.
What I want to know has gone.

The View from Here

With other people's deaths: how everything

has always arranged itself into before

and after. You're a daughter, until you're not.

People like to tell me parenting

is like this, too: a fulcrum over

which your life bends. Your life outside

your body, in your arms. Her name is After,

After. These points on a timeline.

Everything is the same, the same,

until one day you wake up and

what you know, your cells have known before

you, it all sparkles with impermanence,

there is goldengrove unleaving and

you feel the most delicious tingling on

your arm, as it lowers the apple from your lips.

Getting Your Period at the Water Park

Too much of water hast thou, poor Ophelia

All the ways your girlfriends would jump to shield you.
All that unquestioning equation of blood with shame.
All the way back to your locker for quarters
      to buy a tampon from the restroom vending machine.
All the time spent worrying *what if someone saw the stain*
      while you rinsed your bathing suit at the sink,
      a towel wrapped around your waist.
All the reasons you weren't supposed to buy
      a white bathing suit in the first place
      even though it *made you look tan.*
      Central Florida in the 90s, and you, the sponge:
all your unexamined absorption of what white America
      called beauty. You didn't know it then, but think of
all the ways white adjustment of skin-tone has always been
      about money:
all that powder on european women in the eighteenth century:
      their indoor-skin.
      Then twentieth century foxes: white-skin-made-dark
      by the sun and free time,
all those surfing movies,
all the ways to make leisure show up in the body.
      But you hadn't recognized this water yet,
      back there in the bathroom, and you said
all right, let me finish washing out the damning evidence,
      you knew better than to let anyone see
all the leaks in your body. You were supposed to let the world
      dye your body, but to be very careful
      not to let your body stain the world.
All day long, the worry. And
all the years after. And
all your mistakes. And
all the ways this water pins us down, over and over.
      And all the ways to drown.

Quick-Change at the Lady 'Canes

Here we are in Central Florida,
another away basketball game,
one of the under-enrolled schools outside of town,
a foregone conclusion that we will win,
since the Lady Hurricanes only have seven girls
and at least three of them regularly foul out.
There I was, sitting in the bleachers for
the JV boys' game before ours, making fun
of the school's miniscule cheer squad:
four girls in pleated skirts and pom-poms.

Our own school didn't have cheerleaders;
we thought *this* was *progress*. The year 2000.
We were cool, we knew femme was out—
you were supposed to hate makeup
and make a big show of it whenever the occasion arose.
They'd told us that girls could do anything now,
which meant we had to play sports.
One of the cheerleaders reappeared, dressed
for our game, and hit five 3s in the first quarter,
sweating glitter down the side of her face.

During halftime she was back out on the court
with the others, still in her jersey,
the cheer skirt pulled over the spandex we all wore
under our uniform shorts, and finally I saw:
we were all in the same play
she just had more scenes. After, we had to wait
to share the bus back with the boys' varsity
for whom we had been the opening act.
The sharpshooting cheerleader was back in the front row
with pom-poms, I was trying to do math problems

while my butt went numb on the wooden stands,
back against the cinderblock wall. I was
joining in as my teammates mocked her,

but only because I was scalded whenever I looked
right at her, saw her beaming
while she raised her arms in the air. I'd thought I knew something
about how to be in this world, but there she was
insisting she knew something else, and that was unforgivable.

While Wandering in Montreal, I Mistake Desire for that Feeling You Get When You Actually Want to Be Another Person

If I look at a woman outside this grocery
I won't say waif-like won't say boyish
her shaved head her thin neck
these are words I've been taught
by male writers how can my looking
be different or differently charged
if I still want to look at her body but
all I have are the same old words
here people are speaking in French
which sounds soft romantic
but it's a language of invaders like
English just think how it got here
I got here by driving across the border
from Vermont and also via a violent history
of colonization I am looking
at this woman and wanting
maybe I can turn instead to my own
breath elevated temperature only slightly
where is the border
between wanting and wanting to be
wanting to touch her skin or
live inside it I watch *Killing*
Eve and I think Oh oh I want to dress
up and be someone else oh I want
her to cut me like that

My Younger Self Speaks to Me and I Write Down What She Says

Trace your fever contacts, do what you want,
      I'll sit here stuffing my mouth with hair,
it's all the same: avoiding risk,
      cramming your discourse with someone else's speech,
these are the things that matter.

Yours is still absorbent, I can hear it,
      fewer sources, maybe. Fewer contacts. You're
shrinking.   You're still keenly aware of status, look,
      it's not as if we weren't once that kid
befriending the new girls who transferred in—
      not out of kindness, but from a gambler's sense
that if their status turned out to be high,
      we could hitch ourselves to them.

                        (How can I show you my ugliness without
                        meaning "love me, love me"?)

      Don't look at me like that, I only dulled myself

in certain contexts. Stop it I can hear you
      wincing.   *(Some days it's all my brain can come up with:*
                        how foolish I was. How foolish I was.
                        How foolish I was, how foolish.)
      I can hear you. Is that what you want?
You don't love me yet.

Wanda is a Particle Physicist

Wanda sparkles with curiosity and competence
        and no one underestimates her. The events of her day

are unenraging, and she moves through the physics buildings
        unmolested. Wanda works on things so small

she has to take them on a kind of faith,
        knowing them only by disturbances they leave

in the visible world. *Visible* not quite the word.
        Wanda's computer does what she tells it,

while in a shaft of sunlight in her office,
        some dust motes float, suspended. That she sees them

is certain; they are real. She stares through sunlight
        thinking how it is that love forms an outline

of its object. Wanda looks back
        at the traces her particles have left,

moving through a field.

Star Witness

It helps if you can cry on command.
Go ahead, tell us what you saw.
There are the things we see and the things we don't.
I hear what you're saying, though,
it's hard enough trying to give words
to your own life, and here we are
asking for a door in broad daylight.
I mean the right words
aren't always the answer you think they are,
but tell us the thing we can point to
when we tell you you need protecting.
Haven't you seen enough
to play to your audience by now?
Pay attention to your cues,
look anywhere but at the camera, go on,
tell us there is something out there,
something brooding and
it does not wish us well.

Enough

They're making movies about the handsome serial killer again
as if we've crossed the arbitrary threshold
of enough time I keep seeing just enough of the preview
every time I open Netflix before I can click away
to remind me of my twitching vulnerability in a public place
Look at him these movies say look
how he doesn't look like the thing you'd expect
look how white how blue-eyed how winning his smile
don't we know by now this is what monsters
have always looked like The math is always all wrong too
too many dead women frozen smiling in yearbook photos
listen to his voice on these tapes the movies say
how normal how chillingly normal Fall
in love again they say kneel in fascination
Repulsion looks like worship from a distance or
with the sound turned off Stop
there's too much telling here you can Google
the details yourself but isn't that the point of fame
Think of the orchid mantis Disguise
is life's second-oldest invention No think
what it means to keep telling this story
the story of the wolf in sheep's clothing
is never about the sheep if it were we wouldn't tell it
When I lived far away from that person I used to love
some days I'd go get a cheap haircut just to feel
someone touch me From the other room
I can hear the showerhead do that thing
where it suddenly releases a small final flush of water
half an hour after I've stepped out of the shower alive
Things are never over Think of the volume of insect venoms
your body has absorbed in your lifetime Think of how skin
glues itself back together after you slice your finger
chopping an onion Not scar as metaphor no
how long it takes How quick the knife
The problem with children is that if you're lucky

they grow up I used to go to bars to tame
a swelling need A little suggestive attention
in dim lighting would do it sometimes This is how
the movies tell us to do it because what else
could possibly thrill us but to see the handsome raptor
in the corner of someone's eyes someone
we don't know Of course the problem of other minds
who do we ever know But naming it's no inoculation against
what happens in every parking lot alone at night that memory
rising from deep in my cells   wading upright through
waist-high grass   wingshadow   talons

Substance and Accident

The blood had already dried and the crowd
was starting to disperse by the time someone came
to collect the body of the dead alligator
that had plodded out into one of Alachua County's
busiest intersections an hour before. There it was,
lying there like a fact.
Biggest one in years, people were saying,
shaking their heads or leading small girl-children away,
letting the boys gape a little longer,
because in central Florida this
is how it's done. Animal Control
monitors the swamp-puddle of a reedy pond
a block from downtown, relocating
the occasional gator that manages
to survive in the fuzzy water long enough
to grow bigger than a few feet, but this one
must have hidden out for years, breaking
the surface only with its marble eyes and nostrils.
Let's not speculate about what
might make a six-foot aquatic lizard suddenly
haul itself right out into the open after
so much growth below the muck.
Let's not linger on the image of the skull,
flattened and leaking on the road after
the Honda's driver either didn't see it, or did.
Oil and gore, pooling in patches on the cement.
It would go viral, surely, with the right image
of only the tail sticking out, wet-leather-green,
from behind the traffic cones. It had taken several adults
to drag it out of the intersection by the tail
while we waited for Animal Control, a streaked stain
marking our efforts. I was sweating
as much as everyone else,
everyone looking in the same direction,
or looking away on purpose. This is the same world

it's always been, where lumbering monsters
emerge after years of silence
to take up space and give us pause.
We gaze at their bodies and wander away
to buy groceries, which is fine. I am not talking
about myths or human impact. Not about
identifying with an ancient predator
that slides among us. Not about sympathy
or symbolism. I am talking about disorientation.
About pausing on the hot sidewalk
to look at the ruined body. About spectacle.
You can look, or you can look away, and who am I
to tell you what to do with your monsters?
You can leave them on the road
and walk home without having taken a single photo.
You can wash your hands. You can make dinner.

Dead Ringer

The news breaks while I am on the train
and a woman my age is trying to gently lead
an older woman, who must be her mother,
away from me while the older woman is trying
to tell me how much I look like the dead sister
she has mistaken me for—

all this the younger woman, complete stranger,
explains to me by pretending I'm not the audience
as she says to her mother *Elsa died in 1989, it's*
2019, let's not bother this complete stranger—

Meanwhile I have glanced down at my phone
to finish reading the headline about another
gunman—*She has trouble with time,*
the younger woman says, finally looking
at me. *She can get caught in a loop.*
Maybe my memory is full, the older woman says.

I am trying to smile and nod kindly, but I need
to text my friend who lives in the shot-up city in the news—
Are you ok? I text her *It's on the news here*—

Which is to say *I hope you are not included*
in that headline number, ___ confirmed dead.
Which is to say *I hope it happened to a complete*
stranger instead. It's incredible, the older woman
is saying to me, her small hand gripping a seatback,
you look just like her.
                                    Sorry,
the younger woman mouths to me. *Don't worry,*
I tell them, looking down at my phone, waiting for
the blinking ellipsis to appear which will mean
my friend is alive. Maybe my memory
is full; I am momentarily paralyzed by considering
what to delete so I just refresh the news page, over

and over. When I let the screen go dark, I can see
my reflection. The train rattles. The older
of the two women keeps shaking her head and repeating,
you look just *like her. Just*
like her—

[Once when we were walking, winter,]

Once when we were walking, winter,
she started to bleed, our child.
(Don't worry, there isn't any child)
But the wound was in her leg, deep,
and ragged as a gash from an animal claw.
(As I said, we've never had a child)
It was winter, and we were way up the trail,
so we kicked into the crust of snow
and packed her wound with ice,
a pink slushie of emergency—
then hoofed her down the hill
between us, silent as she always was.
(Children are made of risk, and I am
too broken-hearted already, you knew this)
The day went quiet, fluent in the grammar
of emergency, and the sun sank,
she blinked in the thinning light,
and closed her eyes (you knew it
when you looked at me that night
and said *let's try, let's love something new*).

Fuck, Marry, Bury: Loneliness, Solitude, Isolation

Bury Isolation in the backyard, because
Loneliness wants you several times a day,
can't get enough, wants you
on the kitchen counter, wants it
in the middle of lunch, screw
the workday. And yes, Loneliness
is a great lay, what's more,
will hold you all night, after.
Will drag you back to bed when you try
to get up to make breakfast.
Loneliness will partner all your meals
even though you haven't asked, which
is why they are the Fuck, the number
you can't bring yourself to delete,
the siren of your darkened hours,
though you'd married well when you said
Solitude, thinking of years ahead
to spend in mind, such
quiet years and slow, years and years to pass
unlearning our first native language, touch,
and how it is the body that dies last.

Reader, I Married Him

And the first one who thought I was pretty enough
to give him a blowjob in the parking lot after school.
And the one who still wanted me so bad he kept texting
in the middle of the night for months after I left.
And the one who punched walls, but never me.
And the one who slept around even after
I found out and was cool about it. And the one
who told me he was sure about me because
someone had given him the advice to *look at the mother
to see what she'll look like later.* Reader,
I yielded for years, it was in the script
they handed me in high school. Where are my manners?
Your certainty makes me lonely, but sure,
stay and have something. A drink.
Some leftovers. My attention. I just have to take care
of something first, in the other room, a revision,
revise: I threw the book at him and slammed
the door on my way out. In a poem I can leave
when I should have. I'm off-book. I can make it
so I didn't avert my eyes from all the signs, write myself
the blazing final speech, split myself apart from her,
peel myself out of her skin and walk away.

ShamWow

I am undercover at the grocery store.
I am behind enemy lines and the line is adulthood.
I am standing here, pretending I am not
a child teetering on stilts under a giant overcoat.
Do you ever have trouble finding your dead letter drops?
No, probably not, you *are* the cover, there's nothing under,
the way you talk here is the way you talk in real life,
but I have to pretend to mean things all the time.
Pretend that I feel at home in this life,
say convincing things like *I'm going home now* and mean
the place where I live with a man who scares me. I can't remember
why it matters so much to wake up at the right time
but I have to do it with gusto just like my many colleagues.
I have gone to the grocery to fill in the gaps in my backstory.
I am standing in the home goods aisle asking myself
how much copper plating do I need in my kitchen
to shore up my cover? Will this shatter-proof
plastic stemware give me away for the broken-hearted child
I really am? I am standing holding an apple corer, realizing
they don't have anything I need here.

Something that Floats

The animals visit our lives like the fingers
of a curiosity embodied and hopping,
bolting, lifting away just when we turn
to look.

The year was resuscitating itself
out of frigid wind, the administrators
would say *optimizing new growth.*
I was

taking initiative. I was turning
to look at a frog's throat. No one
listens to women when they're crying.
No one

listens to women unless they're crying,
and then crying can kill. Sometimes
I feel sure I won't have children. On
what honor

do you stake your certainty
that you manufacture
no new harm out of sound?
That year

I learned the common song sparrow
sings a quiet, private copy
of its ordinary song: the *whisper song.*
I learned

because I heard one in our garden,
hopping along the ground to forage seeds,
singing almost inaudibly, for no one
but itself.

Superstitions of the Mid-Atlantic

           No one around anymore
to blame, so, to celebrate,
I set booby traps for myself: a glass of water left in the dark hallway
to kick and spill later, the chair I neglect
to push in, precarious leftovers in the fridge—

All those frozen waffles cleared out
with our daily misunderstandings. An indulgence
to have the place to myself after all this time.

The text didn't send, or *fired*
became *Friday*, an attempt at *airplane*
reduced autoincorrectly
to *apples*, and now here we are thinking about temptation again.
You can come out now, I say to no one.

There were never any good exit strategies anyway.
You've gone missing or I've mis-
placed you like the ritual thank-you letter we received
from your mother after her visit and which I left in the entryway mailbox
to convince the neighbors we weren't home. I still don't know

what you meant when you said *paradise*
out loud when we were eating oranges.
Now when I am in the kitchen eating peaches I say *paradise*.

Show/Tell

Lotte, 5, hides in the corner when you arrive
at the house in Vermont—family friends who remember

you at Lotte's age.
Just a routine visit.
You play the part, smiling
when they ask "How's ————?
We're sorry he couldn't make it tonight."
Your lines are well-rehearsed
but the short-legged dog, Romeo,
seems to sense something and so remains
prone at your feet all during dinner.

(A rescue. He wouldn't answer to anything else!)
Late spring, coming on summer

so the evening lingers in the driveway.
Gravel underfoot, you walk down
the drive to see the chickens as an excuse
to remain enfolded in the cool coming
out of the dip in the hills,
the conversation about the film festival on campus,
their uncomplicated attention. In the meantime,
Lotte has collected backyard artifacts
in the form of beetles, stray leaves, a feather.
(You hold out your hand on command.)
Look at this, she says.
And this.
And this.

Divorced Invertebrate

The year I became a lobster I clacked when I walked.
As a lobster I waved a claw in the air at people I knew

though as a lobster I could see only movement.
No one recognized me, anyway.

Such a short marriage, and already I didn't mean things out loud anymore.
Becoming a lobster only hurt at first,

when the extra legs began to poke through like baby teeth.
As a lobster I became expensive and ugly.

I sank down to the cold bottom.
I lived in the silt and waited to molt the old life off me.

When I saw that the new life was coming in as before,
I decided to stop being a lobster. I slithered out of the rocks

and up into the light, where I didn't recognize anything anymore
and the sun shone on, as required,

and my body was just as mine as if I'd chosen it.

Eve Signs the Papers

A wedding has a script, but marriage
is long-form improv. And scene.
I've lost my sunglasses and false nose somewhere
in the car, but I don't need to play that part anymore,
I'm no longer called upon to say *yes* to everything.
I've moved my mattress to another chamber,
drawn back the shades. An airing out
post-grievance-airing. Yes, I'll stay here;
I've rearranged the furniture in every room.
The rooms are full of plants: olive, philodendron,
ivy vine I refuse to prune, allowing it instead
to scale the doorframe. Here I sit, knife
balanced across one thigh, leaning back, savoring
this apple and cheese. You can see
yourself out, can't you? The sun is streaming in.

Wanda Vibing

Wanda has moved beyond collisions and is looking
      for vibrations. The lab's cat makes too much static,

so they nudge him gently past the door.
      Wanda thinks about what cats are for—

this one doesn't prowl the courtyard or hunt
      the building's mice, but reposes in a patch

of sun, its ease reverberating off the walls.
      At her computer, with a soundtrack made of distant light,

Wanda isn't taking any calls because she's listening
      with headphones to the murmur of it all—

My Younger Self Speaks to Me and I Write Down What She Says

If I hold down the button
for long enough, we can start again.
There are buttons made of possibility.
Look, here's another plate. No,
it's family-style, meaning fight
your sister for the drumstick, bend
a bone like you're drawing an arrow,
draw yourself into the picture.
I'd like to be Artemis,
instead, am Madame Boeuf
sitting here consuming leftovers,
a consummate lover of artifice.
What waste before us now, what
thrills. I want reasons I can dip
in ketchup. We'll eventually see
behind the curtain, won't we?
Don't look at me that way, you're still
built on validation, though I can't quite
see you through the years.
I know where I'm going, but tell me,
did we get there?
You don't love me yet.

Still Life

This, too, is weather. The air
      full, invisibly, of messages
that matter so much we encrypt them.

No matter but an echo. Someone else's
      station. *Hold still.* You may look
at the screen next to yours. The windowsill

in your pocket. Go on.
      The horse will trip the shutters, fly.
To capture (an image). *To take* (a photograph).

Screen grab or *shot.* A hostage lexicon instead
      of sight. I can walk
through air that says *running late* or

LOL or *yes,*
      she is. I can wait
longer these days. You may look

tired. The apple on the windowsill.
This natural light, the de rigueur
draping of cloth.

I am learning how to be a witness.
I am learning how to be
a clock. Everywhere, everyone practicing

their talk. *Help, angels, make assay.*
      I am learning how to tick
to you and learning when

to stop. (I'll bring my bike over on Sunday—
you can help me true the wheel.) *Hold
still please.*

If a Lion Could Speak, We Couldn't Understand Him

World: even when we think we've got it tamed, something:

a hoard of bees on a hot dog stand swarms

so thick the police rope off Times Square at midday!

(resist the temptation, here, to say "the bees want"—

let wild be wild). It isn't less and less,

it's not decay. The smell of hot dogs

in the humid heat. What does a segmented body

know? What it wants? No,

wants is the wrong word. There isn't

a right one. These intrusions,

what do we want them to tell us? *Tell*

is the wrong word. More often it's dead

deer by the side of the highway, full-

grown mammals flinging themselves

into our paths, our way. What is it

that visits us at night, on darkened wings?

Sing is just our word for life as sound,

unbowed. If I have to, I'll find

comfort in those images

in post-apocalyptic movies:

vine-obscured traffic lights, tall

grasses billowing in the intersection

of Lexington and 54th. Time

and moss can crumble a building. Coyotes

on Hollywood Boulevard. When we're gone,

think how the insects will sing.

Late & Soon

Oh, it is good to be among the living,
buying the things the living buy,
doing things to get money, &
waiting for traffic lights to change.
Yes, it is good that there are things
to want & things to want to eat,
deli meats & soft cheeses, bring them
with you to another apartment
where someone else lives.

There's the matter of picking a place
to live. The storms, yes, the heat,
sure, the fires, ok, ok,

but it is good, remember, good
to sit behind the wheel of a car
when you need to eat, to open
the packages that arrive at your doorstep,
good to watch the packaging go away
in a truck, there are scissors for that,
& a schedule, & words to say
when someone reaches out to hand you
a sandwich you paid for—

I'm not betting on anything.
I'm inoculating myself against
hope, dipping myself in a vat
of its opposite till it shines on me
like a coat of lacquer. I walk
out into the sun, gleaming.
It is good. I am saved.
That orphaned glove on the sidewalk
won't break my heart. It won't.

Gig Economy

I am a person you can pay to outsource
the in-person trolling of your long-distance nemeses.
On Monday, I got paid enough to buy a sandwich
for side-eyeing someone at a coffee shop. Yesterday,
it was knocking someone's ice cream onto the sidewalk
and then yelling "Mike says *have a great day!*"
while I made my escape. Today I have a pricey one.
Enough money for a fancy meal to call and cancel
Ubers until my client's nemesis picks me up,
then boo them while they drive me
a single city block, at rush hour.
It can be hard to maintain a constant,
seething rage from a great distance. Outrage
is knee-jerk, but rage is personal. I provide
an important service. The app makes sure to warn users
about how revenge can never satisfy.
This is for legal reasons. For revenge to work,
memory has to work too, and we don't yet have
the technology to remember. I wanted to hurt him back
for so long, wanted to make him feel my exact injuries,
but by the time I had the knife, it turned out it was for cooking
and making instead of cutting, the point
somehow had nothing to do with him.
As for you, better angels, it's either you
or the moon landing. These days I come home at night
and lie next to someone I like.
What are the small, true things we can tell each other?

The Problem of Where to Put Things

Say your uterus is killing you.
Say that phrase is literal,
or call it chronic, knife-point pain.
Say someone says *hysterectomy*,
and then you have to change
your plans, the size and shape
of your life, empty out the rooms
in your imagined future. The future
that once galloped freely, ranging
across all the hills of your mind,
now it limps and you have to pen it.
Remove the pain from one vital part of you
by subtraction. Say you have to make
such a decision, make preparations
in the mind, even if you have someone
to drive you home.
The organ, though, the empty,
hurting house—you have to
let them cut it out. And
the imagined children, the version
of your life that branched away,
some time ago, from where you now
survive, do you just cut that off? No, you do it
like you shoot a beloved, dying horse.
Whispering softly to it,
you lead it gently down
into the horse-sized hole you dug,
then fire.

Taxonomy

It is summer in the fake-sounding year 2020, and
there are a number of names for the various
and invisible ills that infect this country,
keeping us apart, suffocating, but my lover
has discovered birding and suddenly
there is magic everywhere, for him.
The retention pond, for example.
My dog is unhelpful, but I bring him anyway.
There is a toxic algae blooming in New Jersey,
so the water is off-limits to dogs.
He stands, panting, next to me,
while my love peers through binoculars at
a small, dun bird in the reeds that he names, but
I can't tell from all the others. I've lost
my capacity for wonder, these months, I've let
my mind wander further into traps
I set myself. On top of everything else,
there is an invasive insect species
making its way up the coast, destroying
fruit trees. We've seen the photos online,
we're supposed to crush it if we see one:
flecked, linen-colored wings
with bright-red gashes as it flutters.
It's beautiful, and terrible, terrible and beautiful,
like all the beautiful and terrible things
that are dying all around us. *Spotted Lantern Fly:*
even the name is beautiful. Someone we sort-of-know
passes by and waves from a safe distance.
All my love is here, tied up in these two mammals
still breathing next to me, and even that
feels like sticking a limb out into traffic.
It is evening when we get home, and safe,
and one day I will learn that joy can whither
if you hoard it, will learn to name, too,
the things that don't destroy us.

Request for Repair

Now we can enter the phase of life
that feels like that point in the movies when
someone is always saying *I'm in*
I've hacked into the mainframe and
it's true, we've done it this time,
the code was so simple all along,
look, there are the streaming ones and zeros,
we know about the effects of ambient light,
we know we're supposed to feel analog relief
at a dimming, and so we do, mostly.
The dishwasher hums and whispers. Relief,
like a promise kept.

If you've done the update, you'll see
a bar in top right corner that will allow you
to shift tracks. There are two versions
of this game. Some days we play retro.
Sometimes there are birds at the window
and we don't notice. It's a game
about perception and we always lose.
Miraculously, in this version,
you can almost always tell that your hands
are your hands. This version, full
of the minutest miracles and no one knows
how to set them off.

Disaster A/version / Re/vision

In one version, the evening is hot and I ride
my bike to the grocery for emergency
garlic replenishment, waiting carefully at each stoplight
until my phone buzzes in my pocket—

in another, it rains and I take the bus downtown to meet L
and my phone rings on the way home—

Sometimes the dog at the corner barks as I pass—

Sometimes I miss the bus and call L for a lift—

In one version I drive all the way to Fernandina
when I'm just supposed to go to the DMV on 39th,
and it's on my way home that the call

interrupts my music, this could go on,

> and it is always evening when I answer, always just before

> dark as the phone rings, the word *accident*

> from the tinny speaker always sharp as cut
> glass, there I am, always

> lifting the phone to my ear [in the fading
> light], [looking

> straight ahead into a small gust of wind]

Grief is a Sudden Room

Grief is a sudden room.
After flailing around, breaking
all the furniture inside it for a time,
you can think you've shut
the ancient door behind you as you left,
but the latch hasn't worked for eons,
it will just spring open anytime
you open a window, elsewhere
in your mind. No matter. The room
will arrange itself in your absence
and wait for your return.
You've never seen such patience.

Transmission Received from Penelope in Deep Space

We've been [   ] long enough
for my hair to grow past my shoulders.

[   ] pushed off without thinking, of course
[   ] no choice. Survival

at the cost of [   ]
[   ]. We're a message in a bottle now,

and it looks like the Sci-Fi channel promised
it would, only dirtier [   ] ship. Everyone

[ ] top of each other.   The light is so thin, but
we [   ] . Outside [   ] bubble

of radio waves [   ] human voices
from our [   ], so much silence.

I know [   ] gone, but my body is still
in love. [   ] wander [   ].

The word *day* no longer means anything,
but I remember so much.

The sound of insects. [   ] pull
of the earth [   ] my body, like a magnet.

Wind. How I tried to keep even a soft rain
from wetting my skin. [   ].

Memory Palace

Build yourself a palace in the mind. Name the entrance hall for your sister, and in it place your area code, zip code, your mother's phone number.

In the drawing room, put the faces of your students. Sketch them in pencil, so they can age, so you can still find their names on the tip of your tongue, years later.

In the British Isles, one consequence of massive drought is that old land scars become visible again from the sky. Ancient divots made by long-gone huts and stone circles collect slightly more water in the soil, and those patches spring up greener than the parched surroundings. What you see from above is a green outline of a memory.

I worry a lot about memory, but it's stored all around us. My mother. Her father, deep in dementia. He would come back to himself only while listening to music. Suddenly call her by name after months of thinking she was his sister. No, leave the stereo on. Turn it up.

Have you pried open your electronics lately? Have you seen the switchboards? Miniature landscapes of order and design, tiny cities out the plane window. So much mysterious surrounding green. Copper wiring carrying more than you'll ever know.

Did I tell you about the graveyard I pass on my runs? Right there smack in the middle of those fields, a mile from the river, most of the headstones so weathered there's nothing left to read. And this, in America, where we dance on so many graves.

American surnames erase, erase. Whole columns of women disappear from the record under the editing pen of marriage.

Or bear the name of their great-great-grandmother's enslaver. Some of the mansions still stand. You can pay to enter them. Or to be married on the grounds. Dancing.

Already my students, born in the early 2000s, don't remember a time before the internet.

There are dead-end web pages out there in the aether, ghost places frozen as last left, their maintainers absent like the clockwork god. You can stumble on them like ruins, hermetically sealed rooms.

Imagine an eternal surveillance camera in a cave: A flurry of human activity. Imagine it sped up: people racing in and out with torches, hands on the walls, dancing, shapes and lines appearing, bison and lions, horses, handprints. Then, nothing, for 30,000 years: silence and darkness. And the last two seconds of the tape would show two modern cavers stumbling in, having rolled aside the landslide's work. Holding up a flashlight. Falling to their knees.

An alien on route to earth would first hear our voices 113 light-years away, as radio waves. We will sing into the dark, I think, until darkness is all there is. "I Say a Little Prayer," 294 trillion miles away and counting.

Wanda in the World

In the coffee shop near campus, Wanda sits
    with an undergraduate who tells her she finds

the outdated technology of her own body ridiculous;
    she would prefer to be a mind downloaded

on a fancy computer. That's the student's phrase,
    outdated technology, and Wanda remembers wanting

to erase the leaky vessel in which she moves
    through the world. Now Wanda thinks of biting

into a plum's taught skin, and pizza labeled
    Lust auf Fleische from the conference in

Berlin last year. Wanda dwells deliciously
    on her own incarnate-ness, en-meated, in the flesh,

her urgent, near-medical need to reach out and touch
    any textured surface, her lover's skin,

velour, and sure, snakes. Wanda wants to pause and smile,
    sing the body to this student, but she knows

it's really just her younger self she'd make her case to,
    here, today, and Wanda knows to let young people

love the world in their own way.

After

L comes over & we walk turns around the block—
This is what we're allowed.

A cardinal appearing, flash of red—
(something she says? *How beautiful?*)—

& this is what beauty is for—
a trap to make us stay.

We leave a mess, don't we.

I repeat her words & it feels
almost like fluency, like belief, almost,

almost like love. We're still alive
here. We live on the ground.

On the ground, mostly.

Archimedes, Get out of the Tub

Grief has made me stupid

and I forget to tell my class

The Important Thing they must

remember. I cannot remember

what a dongle is for and words

I reach for take off like birds

from a fence post. I want to pour

my life into a different container,

but it's still river water. Reverse

boatman, suggest my students helpfully.

You have a new memory,

says my phone. Eureka, says the shape

of the space inside me.

Peaches

For Anita

Everything has intentions
of its own, even
this knife. A knife's intention

is to cut, which is what
I am using it for:
cutting this peach

into under-ripe wedges
because either patience
or flies come next,

so here is the knife
filling my hand
with intent so full

I almost cut my thumb
across the two-year old scar
of just such

intentions. The pit
into the plastic trash bag
where it will rot

unproductively.
We're not doing
our best. Intending

to help, your phone
keeps suggesting
you add your mother

to emails, not good enough
to have taken her silence
for absence. The peach

isn't good, but
can you imagine?—
next year there may be

peaches again.

Along for the Ride

Sweet Fears   don't worry
the windshield wipers work
See those flakes in the air
don't worry they're off
somewhere melted   melting
our view will be clear
Look at this exit before us
we don't have to stay
on this grief highway always
look turn just a little
and we can pull over
don't worry   my Worries
don't worry   my Fears
leave the windows
just cracked   I'll run in
and bring you your favorites
news and malaise and some
Cheez-Its for me   Look
I won't leave for long
I know this is just
how you know
how to love me
I'll just be a minute
I promise
don't watch   don't look
I'm going   I'm gone

First, and Then, and Then

We'd watched too much *Battlestar Galactica*
in the weeks leading up to the big anniversary
of the moon landing, so it seemed
like a really minor deal when it came around
and all the news outlets and search engines couldn't
let up about it. Truly impressive things happen
every day, here in the future, like the miracle
of LASIK eye surgery gone right and the lady
down the street who microchipped her dog.
Satellites clutter up the night sky, and we're still
adding to the list of things that can kill us,
but it is a good idea to keep thinking about how
symbolic firsts are orchestrated. I couldn't very well
have done anything other than carry myself
across the threshold of my first apartment all those years ago,
when happiness had seemed as far away as the moon,
which, it turned out, was two days by rocket and also
thousands of years of humanity staring into space.
And anyway, *carry* becomes the wrong verb
for anything other than a tune in both zero gravity
and self-sufficient womanhood. Whether we know it or not,
the world has already handed us our lines
for when we come to grief, though method acting is optional.
Me, I've been gathering reports of people
whose second lives have bent toward joy.
Look at you, here, in my life, the machine
of the world that set us in orbit together,
my astonishment undimmed by the daily sight of you
entering a room. Or the sound of your whistling
carrying through the door.

The Clearing

I treat happiness
like the half-tamed deer I have coaxed
into a clearing and want only
to be near—
If I look right at it,
it will spook and disappear.
Instead I have to look studiously
away, offering my mind permission to marvel
only out of the furthest
corner of my eye.

If I reach out to it with a handful
of something sweet,
it will smell a trap and start
away, flash of white tail
into the underbrush.
No sudden movements.
I only want
to look at you. Stay,
just long enough
to let me look at you in the fading light.

At the Tolstoy Museum We Sat and Wept

We're here now, so let's take inventory: now there are these women pulling off great heists in the movies, and I've gotten better at avoiding places where I'll be cloaked in a scent-cloud of someone else's perfume. Pause there, before this list gets into the real depressing parts. Oh! I just want to type out Frank O'Hara poems and look at my dog, but let's not kid ourselves about the innocence of teeth. There are lots of places I want to go and others I want to avoid and you can get a bag of potato chips near all of them. Come with me. Bring that album and we can talk over the skip-tracks. Oh, leave the door. The rain's coming in through the windows anyway.

Civilization VI

I have set all my Great Artists to sleep
because I have nowhere to put their Great Works.

This world is made of a number of hills and some tundra.
The Barbarians are hanging around

into the Eighteenth Century for some reason,
but Rome still gets a roads bonus. In this version

of the game, Cleopatra has built the Eiffel Tower
and is winning in Space-Race Points, but I

have recruited Shakespeare, Basho, and Emily Dickinson.
My dog sits next to me, sure the world is made

of soft places for him to lie on. Shakespeare is sleeping
in Paris, waiting until I finish building

him the Bolshoi Ballet. My friend is sleeping it off
in the next room, spaced out, too game.

We made a mistake together once. We're good at this.
Making mistakes. Wasting time. I do a lot of both.

I'm bad at sleeping, good at lying down.
Out here there's an island of three million

citizens without power or water, which isn't in the game.
I named my dog a palindrome for no good reason.

I wake him up, saying his name, just to see him
look at me. We're good at this. It's good work

to tire out a dog or to sit with a sleeping friend.
This one lives far away but needed a place tonight.

We both know there's no Eve here, just . . . A dog! A panic in a pagoda!
I've told you all this before, but I have nowhere to record it.

Works to write it down, but my friend, who just moaned,
is sleeping with my notebook. It won't be long

before we build the version where memory works
and all roads lead to home.

Fuck, Marry, Bury: Speaker, Poem, Poet

Of course I am trying to bury myself

deep in the hole I have dug
with this keyboard, but that same self

is trying so hard to merge

with me we might as well be fucking.
Come here, darling. Let's live together

in this room we have built.

Garden State

The world smells green & wet & today I
am in a postlapsarian good mood
as I meander by the Raritan canal,
no longer moving in a deadly torpor
like a winter fly, but thinking once again
(the warming weather) about sex in a good way,
how all those smells you're supposed to be ashamed of
or wash away smell *good* once you know a thing or two,
& it's finally humid enough, this second day
after the rains, it is spring in New Jersey,
I itch my eyes freely & blink down on gnats
that seem determined to die in my field of
so-close-I-can't-see-them, & people are out,
look at all their beautiful bodies, so many
ankles & knees, clicking whizz of bike wheels,
car exhaust hanging in the thick air,
helmets pressing sweaty hair to sticky foreheads,
a racket of motors on the other side of these trees,
early evening: the light just now is furtive, holy,
this is no prologue but the thing itself, the mud
& the grease & the grass & the wet asphalt
on one of those steaming, streaming, sunlit evenings
after a week of rain that brought out the frogs
to cover the road up the hill. There they were.
No one knew where they were going.

At a Distance

Entanglement (Quantum Physics): a phenomenon in which particles remain connected so that actions performed on one affect the other, even when separated by great distances. The phenomenon so riled Albert Einstein that he called it "spooky action at a distance."

Wanda leaves her nail polish in the photon lab
        for the seventh time this term. Redshift Red

it's called, the color of receding. The Cavendish
        is cold this time of year, but news

from the University at Delft is of entanglement.
        Even while she reads the memo, Wanda thinks

instead of what a color knows of cues:
        Blue knows about announcements like approaching light.

In that other Delft school, how Vermeer's
        windows annunciate this daily

miracle—whispered assurances
        of how little we know, or what remains unsaid:

A woman holding scales, receiving letters,
        or just attending to the milk and bread.

NOTES

↖ is the meteorological symbol for a thunderstorm. In central Florida's monsoon season, you used to be able to set your watch by the daily, short-lived afternoon thunderstorms.

Wanda is an invention. At worst: an aspirational alter-ego, at best: a 21st century patron saint of curiosity and wonder.

"Haunt" revises some lines from Robert Frost's "Directive."

"The View from Here" borrows Gerard Manley Hopkins' delicious phrase "goldengrove unleaving" from his poem "Spring and Fall," a poem I've always loved, being, as it is, addressed to someone named Margaret. ("It is Margaret you mourn for," indeed.)

"Getting Your Period at the Water Park" takes its epigraph from *Hamlet*.

Both poems titled "My Younger Self Speaks to Me and I Write Down What She Says" take their last line from a Vulgar Boatmen song called "You Don't Love Me Yet."

"Enough" makes reference to two movies about Ted Bundy that both came out in 2019.

In case it isn't obvious, Fuck, Marry, Bury (also known as Kiss-Marry-Kill, Fuck-Marry-Kill, etc.) is a middle-school era game in which you are presented with three options and have to pick one to have a passionate but short-lived encounter with, one to live with forever, and one to destroy.

"Reader, I Married Him" takes its title from *Jane Eyre*.

"ShamWow" takes its title from a household cleaning product that was advertised on TV infomercials in the late 2000s. You can still find some of the commercials on YouTube.

"Divorced Invertebrate" is after the 2015 film *The Lobster* directed by Yorgos Lanthimos.

"If a Lion Could Speak, We Couldn't Understand Him" takes its title from Wittengstein, and owes a debt to Nicole Sealey's poem "Object Permanence."

"Late & Soon" takes its title from Wordsworth's "The World is Too Much With Us," and is after Cameron Awkward-Rich's "Meditations in an Emergency," a poem I think about all the time.

"Still Life" borrows a line from *Hamlet*, from Claudius at his most desperate moment: "help angels, make assay."

"Memory Palace" is inspired by a poem by my brilliant friend Alexander Manshel that he once read at a reading in a basement pub in England.

"After" is after Jean Valentine.

"The Clearing" owes a debt to Solmaz Sharif's poem "Look," a poem I haven't been able to get out of my head since I first read *Look*.

"At the Tolstoy Museum We Sat and Wept" takes its title from a short story of the same name by Donald Barthalme.

"Civilization VI" owes its title (and the details of its opening lines) to a computer game of the same name.

In "At a Distance," the Cavendish is Cambridge University's physics building & department. The Doppler Effect: light from a source that is moving away from the viewer appears red-shifted as the waves stretch out, while light from a source approaching the viewer appears blue-shifted as the waves compress. (You can observe this same phenomenon with sound, as the pitch of a receding train sounds lower as the wavelength stretches out, while an approaching train sounds more high-pitched because of the compressed soundwaves.) The Delft University of Technology study on entanglement came out in 2015, and was written about in an October 21st, 2015 *New York Times* article by John Markoff titled "Sorry, Einstein. Study Suggests 'Spooky Action' is Real." The Johannes Vermeer (1632-1675) paintings referred to are "Woman Holding a Balance," "Woman Reading a Letter," and "The Milkmaid."

ACKNOWLEDGMENTS

With gratitude to the following publications, in which these poems appeared, sometimes in earlier form:

The Adroit Journal: "Taxonomy," "Haunt";
Alaska Quarterly Review: "Substance and Accident," "The Clearing";
Aquifer: The Florida Review Online: "Grief is a Sudden Room";
Barrow Street: "Freezing the Meat";
Comstock Review: "Dead Ringer," "Enough," "The View from Here";
The Cortland Review: "Archimedes, Get Out of the Tub";
december: "Disaster A/version Re/vision" (runner-up for the *december* Poetry Prize, selected by Carl Phillips);
FIELD: "Tourist," "Show/Tell," "At a Distance," "Garden State";
Frontier Poetry: "If a Lion Could Speak, We Couldn't Understand Him";
The Gettysburg Review: "Civilization VI," "First, and Then, and Then";
Glass: A Journal of Poetry: "The Problem of Where to Put Things";
Gulf Coast: "Expulsion Lessons but Replace the Garden with a Swamp";
Habitat: "Superstitions of the Mid-Atlantic";
LEON Literary Review: "Transmission Received from Penelope in Deep Space," "Along for the Ride";
Michigan Quarterly Review: "Getting Your Period at the Water Park";
Mortar Magazine: "Still Life";
Narrative: "After";
North American Review: "The End of August" (James Hearst Poetry Prize Runner-Up);
Poet Lore: "Reader, I Married Him";
Rhino: "Fuck, Marry, Bury: Loneliness, Solitude, Isolation";
Scoundrel Time: "Gig Economy";
Southeast Review: "Making Out at the Movies";
Spillway: "A Collection of Dangerous Things Interspersed with Things Occasionally Fine or Good";
SWWIM: "ShamWow";
Threepenny Review: "My Younger Self Speaks to Me and I Write Down What She Says";
Third Coast: "While Wandering in Montreal, I Mistake Desire for that Feeling You Get When You Actually Want to Be Another Person" (Winner of the 2020 *Third Coast* Poetry Prize);

The Yale Review: "Hail Mary";
Zócalo Public Square: "Wanda Vibing."

"First, and Then, and Then" also appeared in the 2021 *Best New Poets* anthology, edited by Kaveh Akbar.

"Peaches" was a finalist for the 2022 *Montreal International Poetry Prize.*

Thank you to the editors of *Aquifer: The Florida Review Online* for nominating "Grief is a Sudden Room" for a Best of the Net award.

Some of these poems also appear in the chapbook *Superstitions of the Mid-Atlantic,* from the Poetry Society of America, which won the 2020 Chapbook Fellowships Prize. Thank you to Jericho Brown, for reading, and then seeing something in those poems, many of which also appear here. I still can't quite believe it. Thank you to Brett Fletcher Lauer for everything.

Immense gratitude to Stephanie Burt, for selecting this collection of poems, and especially for her beautiful words about it. To be seen and read by such a poet and thinker is the highest honor.

Thank you to the whole BOA team, and especially to Peter Conners, Gena Hartman, Michelle Dashevsky, and Sandy Knight, for their warm welcome to the press, and for all their amazing design and editorial alchemy and work on behalf of this book. Thank you to the other BOA authors who have been so welcoming. It's the honor of a lifetime to be among you.

In addition to being immensely grateful for all his poetry, I am grateful to Kaveh Akbar for introducing me (in a lecture he gave at Warren Wilson) to the poetry of Jean Valentine, and his thoughts on breakage in poetic (and all) language. I think about that lecture all the time; I am trying to write towards it.

When I was first testing out whether my writing was something I could actually show other people, Linda Gregerson and Corey Van Landingham each offered me encouraging feedback and took me seriously, two great gifts.

Thank you to my teacher Michael Wood, for his model of a life full of reading and writing that means a life full of joy, wonder, and play.

I carry such gratitude for Brenda Shaughnessy, since she offered me advice and kindness and a door when I was at a frantic and clumsy crossroads trying to figure out how to make poetry fit into my changing life. I'm forever grateful for her poetry and brilliance, and to have been lucky enough to have learned from her in person even for a short period of my life, and to go on learning from her work continuously even after I left Rutgers.

Thank you to Deb Allbery, for making such a beautiful space for writers and letting me be part of it.

Deep, deep thanks to Daisy Fried, Sandra Lim, Alan Shapiro, Matthew Olzmann, and Connie Voisine, who all read early (and late) versions of some or many of these poems and made them (and the book) better for their visions and questions. To have such generous teachers is a marvelous gift... I hope to be learning from them my whole life..

Love and gratitude to my Warren Wison cohort of fiercely good, inspiring writers.

Thank you to my pandemic virtual Bread Loaf workshop and Victoria Chang for help with several of these poems; what an inspiration.

Thanks to my English department colleagues in Mem Hall all these years. What an honor to teach alongside you.

Thank you to my beloved first readers of bad drafts, especially Molly Johnsen, Sarah Audsley, and Josh Lopez.

To my brilliant friends and especially D and my family: your thoughts (and your writing) and our conversations are all over everything I think and write. The things you recommend to me to read, watch, listen to, the things we talk about while walking or cooking or sitting...

Thank you again to my sister, Eleanor Ray, for lending her haunting painting to the cover of this book, and for her whole body of inspiring work. I'm always excited to see what you make next, to see how you see.

For my family full of artists. For my father, who always reads to me. For my mother, the music of my life. For D and Otto, my heart.

ABOUT THE AUTHOR

Margaret Ray grew up in Gainesville, Florida. She is also the author of the chapbook *Superstitions of the Mid-Atlantic* (2022, selected by Jericho Brown for the 2020 Poetry Society of America Chapbook Fellowship Prize). Her poems have appeared in *Best New Poets 2021, Threepenny Review, Narrative,* and elsewhere. A winner of the *Third Coast* Poetry Prize, and a finalist for the Montreal International Poetry Prize, she holds an MFA from Warren Wilson College and teaches in New Jersey, where she lives with her partner and a spotty dog. She's on Twitter (occasionally) @mbrrray, on Instagram (for now) @m_rrray, and you can find more of her work at www.margaretbray.com

BOA EDITIONS, LTD.
A. POULIN, JR. NEW POETS OF AMERICA SERIES

COLOPHON

BOA Editions, Ltd., a not-for-profit publisher of poetry
and other literary works, fosters readership and appreciation
of contemporary literature. By identifying, cultivating, and publishing
both new and established poets and selecting authors of unique
literary talent, BOA brings high-quality literature to the public.

Support for this effort comes from the sale of its publications, grant
funding, and private donations.

ß

*The publication of this book is made possible, in part,
by the special support of the following individuals:*

Anonymous
Blue Flower Arts, LLC
Angela Bonazinga & Catherine Lewis
Christopher C. Dahl
James Long Hale
Margaret B. Heminway
Grant Holcomb
Kathleen Holcombe
Nora A. Jones
Paul LaFerriere & Dorrie Parini, *in honor of Bill Waddell*
Barbara Lovenheim
Joe McEleveny
Stephen & Theo Munson
Nocon & Associates, a private wealth advisory practice of
Ameriprise Financial Services LLC
Boo Poulin
John H. Schultz
William Waddell & Linda Rubel
Michael Waters & Mihaela Moscaliuc